Macramé Patterns

A Complete Guide to Design Astonishing Patterns, Give a Stylish Touch to Your Home or Garden and Master Macramé Knots with Illustrated Projects for Beginners and Advanced

Emma Elliott

Table of Contents

Introduction

Macramé is a type of textile making that does not require the conventional method of weaving or knitting, but of tying knots alternately by way of a set of knots. It is believed that it began in the 13th century in the Western Hemisphere with the Arab weavers. They were the first to knot the leftover ribbons and threads at the edges of hand-woven fabrics, such as towels, veils, or shawls with decorative purposes.

What we found fascinating is that sailors were the people who created this attractive knot, and they have also been credited with dispersing this art. They decorated with knots to cover anything from knife handles to bottles and ship parts. Sailors also used them to find something they wanted or when they reached land. Sailors in the 19th century are said to have used the knot to make hammocks, bell fringes, and belts in their spare time to avoid boredom. They referred to the macramé as a "square knot" because it was the knot they used most often.

The materials that are often used for macramé are cotton thread, hemp, thread, or leather. Although there are variations, the main knots would be the fully viable square knot and the double half knots. In jewelry, it is usually developed by mixing ribbons with diamonds, diamond rings, or diamond cubes.

After having been looking at these basic knots that are often used to create macramé, I came across the Cavandoli macramé. This design consists of two colors, one as a background and the other as a drawing, using the double knot or 2 main knots without leaving spaces without weaving, so it is compact. It can be used to make a softer type of fabric that works great for dining table mats, purses, and posts in conjunction with slipcovers.

The name Cavandoli macramé comes from Valentina Cavandoli,

an Italian teacher who won a gold trophy of fame in 1961 before passing away at the age of 97 in 1969. She returned to Italy at the end of the "First World War"; this exceptional lady became the director of a home for rebellious or orphaned children. It is a center where possibly 100 young people between the ages of 1 to 5 were placed. To keep the children busy, she taught them an art she had learned from her great-grandmother: macramé. The children learned how to weave these pieces, which took time, attention, precision, and discipline. The things they created were promoted in marriages and the money raised was put into a savings account for each child, which they could use when they left home.

Enthusiasm for macramé seemed to wane for some time, although it was widely used since the 1970s by American neo-hippies, as well as the grunge public in jewelry production. This art was comprised of handmade anklets and bracelets adorned with handmade glass beads and natural elements such as shells and bones.

Macramé is a fun art to try, and you can start on a very small budget. You may find a host of free or cheap layouts and some how-to guides to get you started. It may be an ideal craft to make your kids, grandchildren, or anyone busy.

Macramé is a crafting strategy that uses knots to create several materials. As this art has regained popularity within the number of decades, both crafters and artists are producing advanced approaches to take macramé beyond the ornamental plant figurines and wall-hangings.

This age-old practice went out of fame for decades. But this technique will likely be open to a degree as a consequence of its own viability. Surprisingly, it is very likely to create things like table runners and key chains with only the hands using a couple of cheap supplies.

In case you want to learn more about how the macramé originated and how to go about starting a job in Macramé, read on.

Why Is Something Macramé?

Macramé is a procedure of making a fabric that utilizes several knots to produce a very straightforward form and role of this product. Each knot is able to be tied with your hands, and then there aren't any tools demanded apart from the routine mounting ring to help keep the merchandise in place while you work.

For something to be contemplated macramé, the project will have a minimum of one macramé knot. Ordinarily, macramé activities are pieced with numerous knots. Every once in a while, you have macramé components combined along with various techniques such as weaving or knitting.

Macramé Desktop

In the modern background, macramé is still an art type of the Arabian countries that attracts the western. Arabian weavers used many knotting ways to complete the edges of woven tapestries, rugs, and shawls with fringe.

As these fabrics were spread through Europe, more people started to test out knotting as a pastime. In the 17th-century, macramé had achieved England where the ladies in wanting were taught under the advice of 'Queen Mary II.'

Women weren't the only real folks practicing macramé. Sailors would knot for functional purposes, however, on extended voyages, the exercise of knotting functioned like a means to keep engaged and reduce the chances of boredom. These sailors finally helped this art spread across Europe. They became merchants once they entered new ports and could swap the

Macramé items, they made on the ship. Popular items contained hats, hammocks, and belts.

Finally, Victorians were knotting fabrics throughout the 18th and 19th centuries before the method was replaced using sewing machines following the Industrial Revolution. The hand-knotting became famous from the late' 60s and 70s' but it was immediately out of fashion in the 1980s.

Knotting - or macramé - is only one of many crafts that are being revived by women and men who love hands-on working. Exactly the same as alloy embroidery, quilting, and needlework are watching with a bulge in fame, macramé was modified from using a 1970s relic to a sexy, trendy art form.

A flexible form of fiber art, macramé can potentially be employed to earn everything from wall-hangings and plant figurines into jewelry, bags, in addition to clothing items. Embellishments such as wooden or glass beads, combined with colored threads, also can open a collection of creating chances.

Learn a bit more about the intriguing background of macramé before diving into fundamental methods and tips to find the very ideal approach to begin creating your own personal or purchasing some contemporary macramé.

Getting Started: What You Need to Know

The Background of Macramé

The origins of Macramé are quite intriguing and have a history that goes back centuries. Some think that the expression comes from the Arab term miasma of century XIII, which means "fringe". Additionally, women and men believe that its roots lie in the Turkish word macramé, which explains "napkin" or "towel" and is still a means of solving the elements of pruning using exorbitant threads around the top or bottom of the woven material.

In almost any case, the decorative macramé seems first followed by the Babylonians and Assyrians portraying braided with fringes used to decorate curtains. From the 13th century on, even Arab weavers used decorative knots to complete the leftover decoration on shawls, veils, and sometimes even towels. After that, it disperses into Europe, throughout North Africa. It is said that moors brought macramé into Spain.

Although many think of macramé to acquire a style from the 1970s, the craft gained fame in England. At the end of the seventeenth century, Queen Mary herself taught classes thanks to her escort ladies. Many Victorian houses had some type of macramé decoration, so it had not been used to decorate clothes, but curtains, tablecloths, and bedspreads.

Considering its ability to create knots, it's no wonder that sailors are largely responsible for distributing macramé around the world. It was a wonderful way to pass the time and could be sold if they were coupled, thus taking you to two areas like China and the new world. Hammocks, straps, side bell fringes are a range of the favorite items made by American and British sailors in the 19th century. Texts like the publication The Royal Macramé Lace from the 1877s goes into detail on different designs and knots, reveal how sexy the procedure had been at that time.

After talking in fame, macramé found a Resurgence from the 1970s. It was found to indicate the bohemian layout and has been useful to get wall hangings, plant figurines, accessories, and clothing. The craft finally succeeds in popularity, but trends are normally somewhat cyclical. Today macramé returns, making waves, creative artisans make modern designs that have revitalized historical knotting procedures.

Handicrafts were always a very fundamental human activity; for, crafts are an integral part of human life. Few crafts such as macramé can prove to be fascinatingly absorbent and flexible. With the textile industry changing rapidly, there is a need to revive and replace the old craft with modern ways in this ever-changing market for newer fashion.

In ancient times, knots and the knotting tradition were closely associated with magic, medication, and religious views for much of history. Knots also acted as bases for mathematical structures (for example, by the Mayans), before writing skills were introduced; and string games and other alternate uses were and are still numerous, of course. All these things have been carried out in one way or another and by all races since ancient times. They are even being taught all over the world nowadays. Additionally, it is safe to say that it will continue to follow until the day comes that humankind no longer exists.

Macramé as an aspect of decorative knots permeates nearly every culture, but within those cultures, it can manifest in different directions. The carefully braided strings, with the assistance of a needle-like tool, became the item for shaping fishnets. Their use in the fashion industry has been spectacular and influential among the youth in making sandals, shoes, jewelry, etc. It is now used also with other products to fashion all kinds of beautiful works of art.

Macramé is closely associated with the trendy youth due to its rapid growth, quick adaptability, and extensive uses. Concerning its use for fashion items, macramé exercised in the textiles became an essential focus on the creation of each decorative piece of clothing, particularly on the fringes of each tent, clothing, and towel. In this, macramé became a synonym for hanging planter. In its traditional forms, macramé (It is an Italian name given in Genoa —its home and place of birth) became one of the most common textile techniques.

Knots are used for the passage of time for several practical, mnemonic and superstitious reasons. Knotting dates back to early Egyptian civilization in Africa, where knots were used in fishnet and decorative fringes. The Peruvian Incas used a Quip, made from the mnemonic knot (Basically, overhand knots) to help them record and convey information. The use of ties, knot size, rope color, and knot both helped to communicate complicated messages. Knots were used in surgery (as slings for broken bones) and in games in ancient Greece (one such mystery was the Gordian knot). In the early Egyptians and Greek times, 'Hercules' knot (square knot) was used on clothes, jewelry, and pottery, which had a spiritual or religious meaning.

The near association between contemporary crafts and macramé has led to the discovery of a range of methodologies and integrative methods, common in most cases, in the content and the adapted techniques. Such advanced methods and integrative techniques reflect the accomplishment of macramé art and its development.

As a product of the artistic intervention of scholarly artisans, this human intellectual accomplishment became necessary to incorporate modern architecture requiring the use of other materials for trendy artifacts. While macramé art has been created and used for onward creation in most cultures aimed at achieving both practical and artistic appeal, their end products vary from one culture to the next. These innovations, however, are, by definition, integral parts of cultural growth and are the results of the macramé artisans' revolutionary accomplishments over the years. The use of adornment knotting distinguishes early cultures and reflected intelligence creation. It is an art that fits all ages and abilities. Today, macramé is experiencing a Revival of the 20th-century. Both men and women transition to work with their hands and build not just utilitarian pieces but also decorative ones.

This simplicity and durability, given the importance of macramé, portrays macramé as just a kind of commodity, described from a noneconomic viewpoint due to its slow production design. Macramé is full of vitality, adaptable, and exploratory and in several respects in product creation and production lends itself for processing and handling. Macramé painting has been a highly valued talent from the earliest times around the world.

The journey of macramé production traveled through Arabia in the XIII century, Turkey, and Spain during the Arab conquest, and spread to the rest of Europe since in the 14th century it reached Italy and France in the early XIV and XV centuries. It was later introduced to England in the late 17th century and mid-19th century in Victorian times.

Sailors and seafaring people are said to have spread this art style all over the world according to tradition. By the 1920s, macramé had reached its dormant period in China and America, making artifacts such as flower hangers, skillfully made boxes, and industrial containers.

Macramé has also proven to be an excellent natural treatment for those undergoing recovery procedures and helps to restore memories once again, making it a unique experience for all. Playing with and tying the ropes, strengthens arms and hands, which helps relax wrist and finger joints. It also helps to calm the mind and soul, as attention is necessary, and the repeated patterns put the weaver in a meditative mood. It is believed that stress is reduced by the fingertips, making macramé knotting a calming task.

Macramé has the added benefit of embracing the self-expression cycle by establishing the underlying purpose concealed within.

Terms Used in Macramé

As you work on different macramé patterns, you may come across words, abbreviations, and methods used in instructions like filler cords, cord holding, fusing, project board, etc.

Here is a list of some simple macramé words, which you need to learn as you follow trends.

- **Row:** A line of knots write next to one another, each bound with a separate working rope.
- **Alternating Cords:** Forming a new set of cords by taking a slice of the cords from previously attached parallel knots, and joining the layers below and above where the cords start.
- **Change Cords:** Changing the position of braiding and filler cords to make the last braiding cords the filler cords and the last filler cords the braiding cords, respectively.
- **Filler Cords**: String in the middle of the knotting cords.
- **Fusing:** Fusion is done with Polypropylene. The process of joining two cords. Hold a lighter butane flame near the ropes, to melt together the fibers. The ends roll between the fingertips. (Wet your fingers to avoid being burned).
- **Holding Cord**: It's one of the most common terms used in macramé. Holding cord is used to identify one or more cords holding and supporting the knots produced by active cords.

- **Knotting board**: It is usually a printed grid fiberboard. It can be used as a clipboard as well, or even a firm pillow, to hold your project up.
- **Wrapping Cord**: Cord used to gather a group of cords and tie them. You can see this on a plant hanger's top.
- **Knotting Cord:** The left and right strings used to form knots over filler cords.
- **Picot:** Loops created by stretching the active cords past the knot a length and then pulling them up to the knot above.
- **Sinnet:** A vertical series of knots bound continuously together, made from the same knot with the same working cords.
- **T-pins:** Metal pins that have a T shaped head. T-pin is used to attach your work to the Knotting Board. To add sturdiness, place the pins at an angle.
- **Working Cords:** All cords in a pattern, those doing the binding (knotting cords), and those wrapped around (filler cords).

Macramé Materials

There are several recognized fabrics used to do macramé. These include silk, rayon, raffia threads, shoe sewing threads, cotton threads, jute, cloth strips, leather strips, shoelace, and all other lightweights, malleable, foldable, and durable, and hand safe fabrics. Yet jute, silk, linen, and cotton are the most common fabrics used for macramé as they tie easily, come in several sizes, can be dyed, and are readily available. Any yarns come with wax, creosote, or scale finish on them. Besides, any material is suitable for macramé, which can be bought in incredible lengths and seems to be pliable. Jute, raffia, cotton, and rayon threads are indigenous to the materials described above.

• **Macramé Cord: Linen**

Linen cording comes in a broad range of colors and sizes that make it highly desirable for many styles of braiding. Linen does have the durability and range that most other cording materials don't have, making it ideal for macramé projects which need to be sturdy and robust. Linen cording is mostly used in wall hangings in macramé and looks fantastic when paired with other cording types, such as cotton and silk. The one thing to keep in mind while macramé with linen cording is that it will unravel very quickly, so one needs to be very sure to finish the project's ends cautiously.

• Macramé Cord: Cotton

Cotton threads are weaker than jute, hemp, or linen and need more bending to allow them to hold together to form a chain. In most fabric and sewing shops, where you work, you can purchase cotton cording or even from weaving suppliers. Single-ply cotton is used for macramé creations that you'll wear, like a shirt. Cotton cording tends to come in a wide range of sizes and is found in many designs of macramé.

Where would the finished piece be used is an essential factor in selecting the bead shape for your project? Is it going to be indoors like a plant hanger? Then you would need something that is fade proof. Are you making a hammock? You will need a material that is soft to the touch.

Knots & Patterns

Capuchin Knot

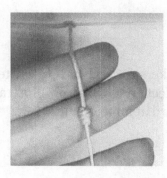

This knot is for any project and can be used as the foundation for the base of the project. Use lightweight cord for this — it can be purchased at craft stores or online, wherever you get your macramé supplies.

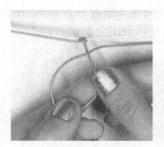

Watch the photos very carefully as you move along with this project and take your time to make sure you are using the right string at the right point of the project.

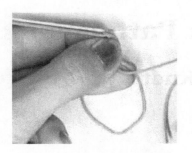

Don't rush, and make sure you have even tension throughout. Practice makes perfect, but with the illustrations to help you, you'll find it's not hard at all to create.

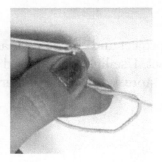

Start with the base cord, tying the knot onto this, and working your way along with the project.

Twist the cord around itself 2 times, pulling the string through the center to form the knot.

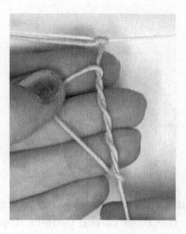

For the finished project, make sure that you have all your knots secure and firm throughout, and do your best to make sure it is all even. It is going to take practice before you can get it perfectly each time, but remember that practice makes perfect, and with time, you are going to get it without too much trouble.

Make sure all is even and secure and tie off. Snip off all the loose ends, and you are ready to go!

Crown Knot

This is a great beginning knot for any project and can be used as the foundation for the base of the project. Use lightweight cord for this – it can be purchased at craft stores or online, wherever you get your macramé supplies.

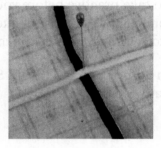

Watch the photos very carefully as you move along with this project and take your time to make sure you are using the right string at the right point of the project.

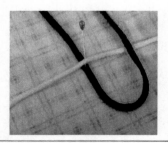

Don't rush, and make sure you have even tension throughout. Practice makes perfect, but with the illustrations to help you, you'll find it's not hard at all to create.

Use a pin to help keep everything in place as you are working.

Weave the strings in and out of each other as you can see in the photos. It helps to practice with different colors to help you see what is going on.

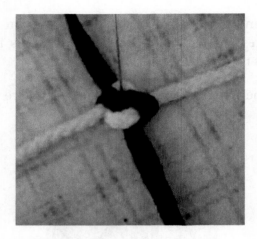

Pull the knot tight, and then repeat for the row on the outside.

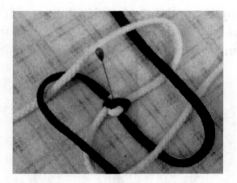

Continue to do this as often as you like to create the knot. You can make it as thick as you like, depending on the project. You can also create more than one length on the same cord.

For the finished project, make sure that you have all your knots secure and firm throughout, and do your best to make sure it is all even. It is going to take practice before you can get it perfectly each time, but remember that practice makes perfect, and with time, you are going to get it without too much trouble.

Make sure all is even and secure and tie off. Snip off all the loose ends, and you are ready to go!

Diagonal Double Half Knot

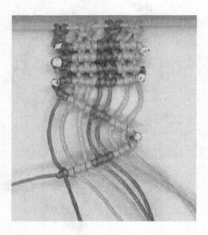

This knot is for basket hangings, decorations, or any projects that are going to require you to put weight on the project. Use a heavier weight cord for this, which you can find at craft stores or online.

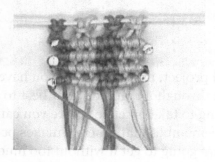

Watch the photos very carefully as you move along with this project and take your time to make sure you are using the right string at the right point of the project.

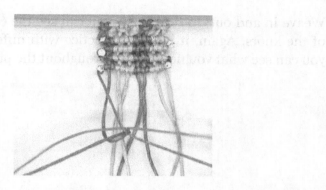

Don't rush, and make sure you have even tension throughout. Practice makes perfect, but with the illustrations to help you, you'll find it's not hard at all to create.

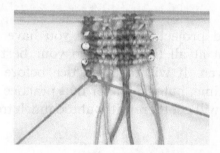

Start at the top of the project and work your way to the bottom. Keep it uniform as you work the length of the piece. Tie the knots at 4-inch intervals, going all the way around.

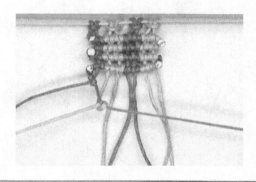

Weave in and out; in the photo, you can see the correct location of the knots. Again, it helps to practice with different colors so you can see what you need to do throughout the piece.

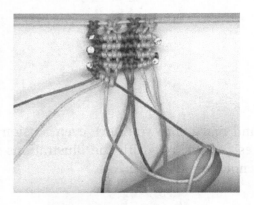

For the finished project, make sure you have all your knots secure and tight at all times and do your best to make sure everything is even. It will take practice before you can do it perfectly every time, but remember that practice makes perfect, and in time you will get there without too much trouble.

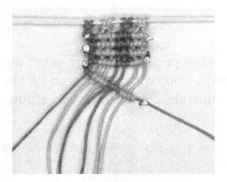

Make sure everything is even, secure, and tie. Cut off all the loose ends and you're done!

Tatting Knot

This is a great stating knot for any project and can be used as the foundation for the base of the project. Use lightweight cord for this – it can be purchased at craft stores or online, wherever you get your macramé supplies.

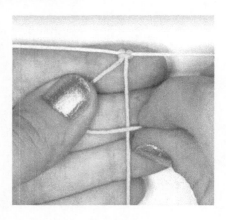

Watch the photos very carefully as you move along with this project and take your time to make sure you are using the right string at the right point of the project.

Don't rush, and make sure you have even tension throughout. Practice makes perfect, but with the illustrations to help you, you'll find it's not hard at all to create.

Use the base string as the guide to hold it in place, and then tie the knot onto this. This is a very straightforward knot; watch the photo and follow the directions you see.

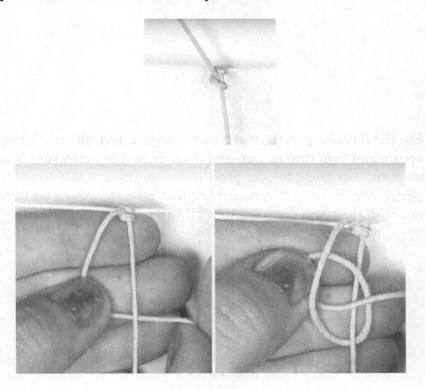

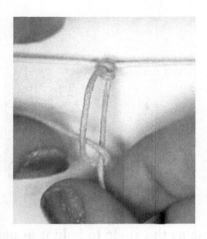

Pull the end of the cord up and through the center.

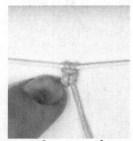

For the finished project, make sure that you have all your knots secure and firm throughout, and do your best to make sure it is all even. It is going to take practice before you are able to get it perfectly each time, but remember that practice makes perfect, and with time, you are going to get it without too much trouble.

Make sure all is even, secure, and tie off. Snip off all the loose ends, and you are ready to go!

Horizontal Double Half Knot

This is a great beginning knot for any project and can be used as the foundation for the base of the project. Use lightweight cord for this – it can be purchased at craft stores or online, wherever you get your macramé supplies.

Watch the photos very carefully as you move along with this project and take your time to make sure you are using the right string at the right point of the project.

Don't rush, and make sure you have even tension throughout. Practice makes perfect, but with the illustrations to help you, you'll find it's not hard at all to create.

Start at the top of the project and work your way toward the bottom. Keep it even as you work your way throughout the piece. Tie the knots at 4-inch intervals, working your way down the entire thing.

For the finished project, make sure that you have all your knots secure and firm throughout, and do your best to make sure it is all even. It is going to take practice before you are able to get it perfectly each time, but remember that practice makes perfect, and with time, you are going to get it without too much trouble.

Make sure all is even, secure, and tie off. Snip off all the loose ends, and you are ready to go!

Josephine Knot

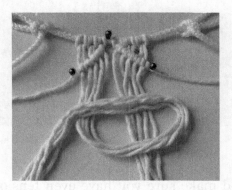

This is the perfect knot to use for basket hangings, decorations, or any projects that are going to require you to put weight on the project. Use a heavier weight cord for this, which you can find at craft stores or online.

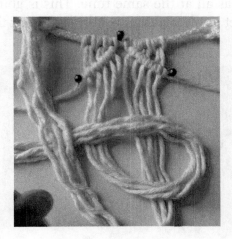

Watch the photos very carefully as you move along with this project and take your time to make sure you are using the right string at the right point of the project.

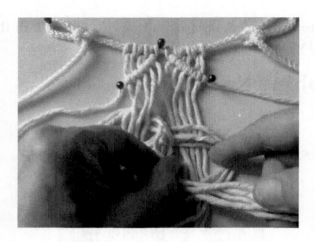

Don't rush, and make sure you have even tension throughout. Practice makes perfect, but with the illustrations to help you, you'll find it's not hard at all to create.

Use the pins along with the knots that you are tying, and work with larger areas all at the same time. This is going to help you keep the project in place as you continue to work throughout the piece.

Pull the ends of the knots through the loops and form the ring in the center of the strings.

For the finished project, make sure that you have all your knots secure and firm throughout, and do your best to make sure it is all even. It is going to take practice before you are able to get it perfectly each time, but remember that practice makes perfect, and with time, you are going to get it without too much trouble.

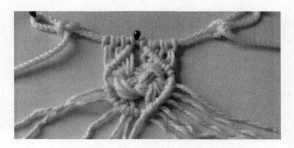

Make sure all is even, secure, and tie off. Snip off all the loose ends, and you are ready to go!

Lark's Head Knot

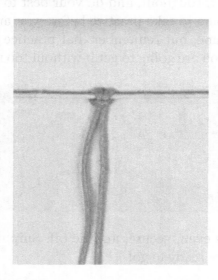

This is a great beginning knot for any project and can be used as the foundation for the base of the project. Use lightweight cord for this – it can be purchased at craft stores or online, wherever you get your macramé supplies.

Watch the photos very carefully as you move along with this project and take your time to make sure you are using the right string at the right point of the project.

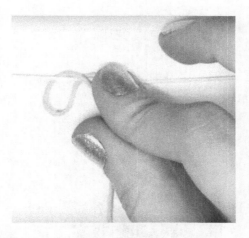

Don't rush, and make sure you have even tension throughout. Practice makes perfect, but with the illustrations to help you, you'll find it's not hard at all to create.

Use the base string as the core part of the knot, working around the end of the string with the cord. Make sure all is even as you loop the string around the base of the cord.

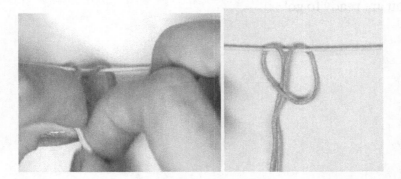

Create a slip knot around the base of the string and keep both ends even as you pull the cord through the center of the piece.

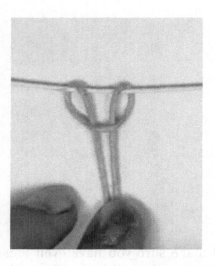

For the finished project, make sure that you have all your knots secure and firm throughout, and do your best to make sure it is all even. It is going to take practice before you are able to get it perfectly each time, but remember that practice makes perfect, and with time, you are going to get it without too much trouble.

You are ready to go!

Tips & Tricks

Whether you're a macramé hobbyist or learner, here are some fundamental tips to help you stay away from mistakes and fully operational in your newfound interest. Knotting is the way to macramé; however, before you start moving, here are some tips that will save you time and dissatisfaction when you are just starting to learn.

Get acquainted with the must-have bunches of the hemp line. It is easy to work and easy to fix the wrong knots.

When you have the fundamental macramé knots down, use nylon cord for your initial gem projects, rather than silk. It is much easier to remove the bind failures.

Burn the tips only works with nylon cords.

Use a simple board as a work area. It's simple to do and you can take it anywhere, making your project portable.

Double-check that the cord you want to use snaps through the bead holes (before you begin!)

To shield the tips from fraying, tie a knot toward the finish of the rope.

You can use clear nail polish on the tips of the rope to prevent fraying as well, and this also stiffens the ends, making it easy to assemble those little seed beads. You can likewise utilize a "no fray" fluid found in textile stores to do the same job.

Save extra pieces of string to test new knots with. The way to achieve a polished look for your piece is to tie it uniformly. Careful discipline produces promising results!

If you don't have any t nails to hand, use corsage pins to make sure about your work. If utilizing calfskin cording, make an x with two pins to make sure about the line set up so as not to cut the rope. Spot the pins on either side of the line crossing in an askew way, similar to an X to make sure about the string set up.

Remember that each of these knots is going to be the basis for the other projects you create, so you will have to take the time to familiarize yourself with each of them and practice them until they are what you need them to be. You probably won't get them perfectly right away, so take the time to make sure you get it right before moving on to the other one.

Don't worry if you don't get it at first, it will come in time and the more time you put into it, the better you are going to become. It takes time and effort to get it right, but the more time and effort you put into it, the better you are going to be.

You see a macramé item, but you look at the price, and you suddenly put it down. You would love to be able to support the artist, and you would love to fill your house with all kinds of handmade and unique items, but when it comes down to it, you simply can't afford to pay those kinds of prices. Of course, it is all worth it, but when you can't afford it, you can't afford it.

However, you don't walk away empty-handed. You now have more inspiration and you know what to do with. You want to make and create. You want to do something that is going to catch the eye of your friends and family, and you want to turn it into something amazing. When it comes to the world of handmade items, you will find that the ways you can show your creativity with the things you make are endless.

If you have creativity, but you don't know what to do with it, and you want to make something, but you feel lost when it comes to the actual execution of the craft, that's where this comes in. In it, you are going to find all kinds of new knots that you can then use to create whatever it is what you want to create. You are going to find that there is no end to the ways that you can use your skills to create whatever it is what you wish.

It can be difficult at first, but the more you put into it, the easier it's all going to become until it is just second nature to you. I know you are going to fall in love with each aspect of this hobby, and when you know how to work the knots, you are going to want to make them in all the ways you possibly can.

Don't worry about the colors, and don't worry if you don't get it right the first time. This is going to give you everything you need to make it happen the way you want it to, and it is going to show you that you really can have it all with your macramé projects.

Wall Hangings

Materials needed for and Macramé Wall Hanging

- Macramé Rope– I have been using this 4 mm rope– 12–16' (as in feet) and cords are required (twelve). Note that this is a thick hanging wall, which is why we need longer cords. To act as your hanger, you will also need 1 shorter piece of cording. Simply tie it on either end with a simple knot.

- A dowel or a stick– I used a long (ha-ha) knitting needle. As long as it is straight and robust and as long as you need to work with what you have!

- Basic macramé knots were used for this wall hanging pattern:

    1. Reverse Lark's Head Knot

    2. Square Knot and Alternating Knot

    3. Half Hitch Knot

Here Is the Step-by-Step Guide for Macramé Hanging Wall

Begin by folding in half your 16' cords. Make sure that the ends are the same. Place the cord loop under the dowel and thread through the loop the ends of the rope. Pull closely. That's the Head Knot of your first Reverse Lark. (For assistance, refer to basic macramé knots). Repeat with the other 11 cords.

First, make 2 Square Knots rows. Now make 2 rows of Square Knots Alternating. Now make 2 more Square knots sets. Follow this pattern until you have 10 rows in total (2 rows of knots in a square, 2 rows of square knots in alternation). Working from left to right, make two half-hitch knots across your piece in a diagonal pattern. Now, from right to left– make double half-hitch knots across your piece in a diagonal pattern. You should have been working your way back to the left.

Keep patterning 2 rows of square knots then 2 rows of overlapping square knots until you have 4 rows in all. Make 2 more rows of knots of a square. We will finish the hanging wall with a set of spiral knots– This is basically a half-square node sequence (or left-side square branch). (Do not end on the right side of the knot, just make square knots and spiral on the left side for you again and again.)

To build this spiral, I made a total of 13 half square knots. Finally– I trimmed in a straight line the bottom cords. The total size for the hanging of my wall is 6.5″ wide by 34.

DIY Round Macramé Boho Coasters

I don't seem to be able to rest every time I find a craft idea until I know how to do that, these coasters are the perfect example, I've done a macramé bracelet before, but to make a macramé round is strange for me. After exploring the internet, I found some confusing posts and made my first coaster when finding ways to create it. That's the way I found it easier (although there's another one I tested as well) and it also got me the most beautiful result.

Supplies:

- 3 mm cotton cord

- Something to hold the cords, a cork coaster or a board, either a tape is useful

- Pins to hold if the cork is used

- Fabric Scissors

- Ruler or measuring tape

- Comb

Boho Christmas Trees

Cut the yarn into 7-8-inch bits. Take two strands and fold them in half to form a loop. Place one of the loops under a twig. Start with the bowed end of the other strand and move the ends of the strand under the twig through the loop.

DIY Bohemian Macramé Mirror Wall Hanging

In the art of macramé, there are so many knots and ways to tie them, it can seem daunting and easy to avoid. I decided to go with a simple project to start my first real attempt. I had an eye on a macramé mirror type plant hanger that I found on Amazon. I would just buy it and call it a day unless I had the resources to make it myself. I used only Lark's head knots, square knots, and some standard basic knots in this project to make things too complicated.

Supplies:

- Macramé Cording: 4 mm

- Mirrored octagon

- 2 inches Wood ring

- Wood beads: 25 mmw/10 mm hole size

- Strong scissors.

Cut 4 pieces of cording macramé of 108 inches (or 3yds). Fold the strips in half and tie all four of them with a Lark's Head knot on the wood loop. Tightly and closely pull the knots. Separate two head knots from the Lark and begin to tie them into a square knot. Start tying into the second two Lark's Head knots two square knots. As you start the second square knot, loop it through one of the sides of the other two knots into a wide square knot. Fasten 7 square knots on both sides. Break the ends after the knots have been tied. Two strings per side and four in the center.

In each of the 2 side cording lines, apply one bead. Tie a knot on both sides under the bead to keep them even. Connect the four cords in the middle to a simple or (overhand knot) about 1/14 inch below the beads. Take a cord from the center and add it to the sides of the two cords. Tie the three on both sides in a knot. Apply the mirror to the end of the knot. Add one of the three sides to the mirror's back to hold it steady. Place clear knots in all 3 side cables at the bottom left and right side of the mirror. Trim the cords again on all three sides. Return one to the back of the mirror on either side and add 2 to the front of it on each side.

Flip the mirror over and tie together all the cords. Flip over the mirror and loosen the knot at the front. Inside the knot, slip the back cords and straighten the knot. Cutting the cord ends up to around 14 inches.

DIY Macramé Bag

What you're going to need

- String

- Scissors

- 2 Gold Jump Ring

- Thread and needle.

We will start by knotting the bag's strap. The length of each string piece must be half the total strap length, time 4. It is necessary that each half of the strap is knotted separately. Our straps should have been defined as a total of 45 cm, so we cut the string pieces half of that time 4. Fold the string in half and use the folded end to knot it on your hoop.

So, you make four knots, take the inner line, loop it around the outer line, and start with the knot on the right. Tighten the knot, and it should look like that. Do the knot, this time using only the string. Use the same knotting method to knot the other side of the belts, this time just reverses the direction. Do these 5 times on both sides.

Again, using the same method of knotting, by extending the knots, attaches the two threads. Repeat three times these extended sets. And change direction and knot for the 3 sets from left to right. Then again repeat the side knots. You've finished half the harness once you've done this! For the other harness and hoop, do this, you will attach them. Do the same knot again to complete the knot work. Snip off one of the knot's threads, and then use the strand to form a new knot. Align the ends and sew together with the needle and thread to attach the straps.

Cut 10 pieces of string four times the desired length of your bag to create the body of the string bag. The bag we made as a guide is 15" (38 cm). Use the folded end as before to knot it onto the gold hoop. The rope bag's body is made with box knots. Starting on the side of two threads, loop it around the two middle strands. Repeat the knot and tighten the knot. Keep doing box knots till you want to have the size of the bag. Twist the end of the strings and drag a little glue into the knots to protect them if you do not want any tassel ends. Remove the bag.

Plant Hangers

Macramé Plant Hanger Beginner

Description: Plant hanger of 2 feet and 5.5 inches (75 cm)

Knots: Square knot, alternating square knot, a half knot, and gathering knot.

Supplies:

- Cord: 10 strands of a cord of 18 feet and 0.5 inches (5,5 meter), 2 strands of 3 feet and 3.3 inches (1 meter)

- Ring: 1 round ring (wood) of 1.6 inches (4 cm) diameter

- Container: 7 inches (18 cm) diameter

Directions (step-by-step):

1. Fold the 10 long strands of cord in half through the wooden ring.

2. Tie all (now 20) strands together with 1 shorter strand

with a gathering knot. Hide the cut cord ends after tying the gathering knot.

3. Make a square knot using all cords: use from each side 4 strands to make the square knot; the other 12 strands stay in the middle.

4. Divide the strands into 2 sets of 10 strands each. Tie a square knot in each set using 3 strands on each side (4 strands stay in the middle of each group).

5. Divide the strands into 3 sets of 6 strands for the outer groups and 8 strands for the group in the middle. Tie a square knot in each set using 2 strands on each side.

6. Divide the strands into 5 sets of 4 strands each and make a square knot with each set.

7. Continue with the 5 sets. In the 2 outer sets, you tie 4 square knots and in the 3 inner sets, you tie 9 half knots.

8. Using all sets tie 7 alternating square knots by connecting two strands in each set with the right two strands of the set to it. In the first, third, fifth, and seventh row, you are not using the 2 outer strands on each side.

9. Repeat steps 7 and 8. In repeating step 8 you tie 5 alternating square knots instead of 7 alternating square knots.

10. To help you with the steps, number the strands from left to right, numbering them no.1 to no. 20.

11. With the 4 middle strands (no. 9 to 12) you make 14 square knots.

12. Make a square knot with the set of 4 strands no. 3 to 6 and the set of 4 strands no. 15 to 18.

13. Divide the strands into 4 sets of 4 strands (ignore the set with the 14 square knots in the middle) and tie 12 square knots in each set.

14. Dropdown 2 inches (5 cm).

15. Make 5 sets in the following way and tie in each set a square knot:

a. Set 1 consists of strands no. 5, 6, 1 and 2

b. Set 2 consists of strands no. 3, 4, 9 and 10

c. Set 3 consists of strands no. 7, 8, 13 and 14

d. Set 4 consists of strands no. 11, 12, 17 and 18

e. Set 5 consists of strands no. 19, 20, 16 and 15

16. Dropdown another 2 inches (5 cm), no knots. This is the moment to place your chosen container/bowl into the hanger to make sure it will fit. If you need to leave more space without knots in order to fit your container, you can do so.

17. Gather all strands together and then tie a gathering knot with the left-over shorter strand. Trim all strands at different lengths to finish your project.

Macramé Plant Hanger Intermediate

Description: Plant hanger of 4 feet and 3 inches (1,30 meter)

Knots: Square knot, alternating square knot, a half knot, alternating half hitch, gathering knot.

Supplies:

- Cord:8 strands of cords of each 26 feet and 3 inches (8 meters), 1 short strand of cord

- Wooden Ring: 1 round ring (wood) of 1,6 inches (4 cm) diameter

- Container/Flowerpot: 7 inches (18 cm) diameter

Directions (step-by-step):

1. Fold 8 strands of cord, the long ones, in half over and through the ring. Now you have 16 strands of cord in total. Group them in sets of four strands.

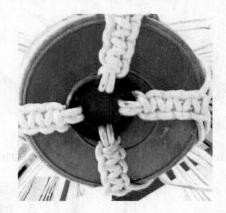

2. Tie 4 square knots on each set of four strands.

3. Dropdown 3.15 inches (8 cm).
4. Tie 4 strands in each set with the right two of the set to it. Repeat on each of the 4 sets.
5. Dropdown 4.3 inches (11 cm).

6. Repeat step 4, starting with the 2 right strands this time.

7. Take 2 strands of 1 set and make 10 alternating half hitch knots. Repeat for the 2 left strands of that set. Repeat for all sets.

8. Dropdown 3.9 inches (10 cm) and tie a row of 48 half knots on each set of four strands.

9. Take the 2 middle strands of each set and make 8 alternating half hitch knots. You leave the 2 strands on the side of the set as they are (without knots).

10. Tie a row of 30 half knots on each set of four strands.

11. Use a new short strand of cord to make a gathering knot around all strands.

12. Cut off and fray the ends as desired.

Macramé Plant Hanger Advanced

Description: Plant hanger of 2 feet and 5.5 inches (75 cm)

Knots: Square knot, alternating square knot, crown knot, gathering knot, and overhand knot.

Supplies:

- Cord: 4 strands of the cord of 13 feet and 1.5 inches (4 meters), 4 strands of 16 feet and 4.8 inches (5 meters), 2 strands of 3 feet and 3.4 inches (1 meter)

- Ring: 1 round ring (wood) of 1.5 inches (4 cm) diameter

- Beads: wooden beads

- Cristal Bowl/Container: 7 inches (18 cm) diameter

Directions (step-by-step):

1. Fold the 8 long strands of cord (4 strands of 13 feet and 1.5 inches and 4 strands of 16 feet and 4.8 inches) in half through the wooden ring.

2. Tie all (now 16) strands together with 1 shorter strand with a gathering knot. Hide the cut cord ends after tying the gathering knot.

3. Divide the strands into 4 sets of 4 strands each. Each set has 2 long strands and 2 shorter strands. Tie 5 Chinese crown knots in each set. Pull each strand tight and smooth.

4. Tie 8 square knots on each set of four strands. In each set, the 2 shorter strands are in the middle and you are tying with the 2 outer, longer strands.

5. Tie 15 half square knots with each set.

6. Dropdown 5.5 inches (14 cm), no knots, and tie an alternating square knot to connect the left two cords in each set to it.

7. Dropdown 3.15 inches (8 cm) and tie again an

alternating square knot with 4 strands.

8. Dropdown 1.5 inches (4 cm). Place your chosen container/bowl into the hanger to make sure it will fit, gather all strands together and then tie a gathering knot with the left-over shorter strand. Add a bead to each strand end (optional). Tie an overhand knot in each strand and trim all strands just below the overhand knots.

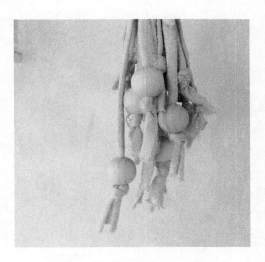

Home Accents

Now, it's time to learn how to make various home decors—simply by using the art of Macramé! Check them out and see which ones you want to make yourself!

Modern Macramé Hanging Planter

Plant hangers are really beautiful because they give your house or garden the feel of an airy, natural space. This one is perfect for condominiums or small apartments— and for those with minimalist, modern themes!

What you need:

- Plant

- Pot

- Scissors

- 50 ft. Paracord (Parachute Cord)

- 16 to 20 mm wooden beads

Instructions:

First, fold in half 4 strands of the cord and then loop so you could form a knot.

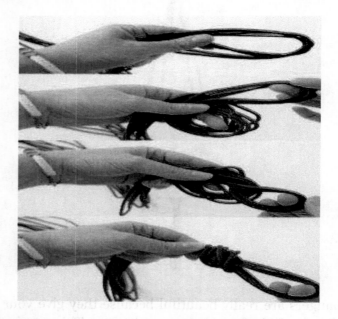

Now, divide the cords into groups of two and make sure to string 2 cords through one of the wooden beads you have on hand. String some more beads—at least 4 on each set of 2 grouped cords.

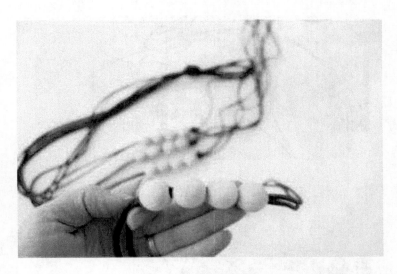

Then, measure every 27.5 inches and tie a knot at that point and repeat this process for every set of cords.

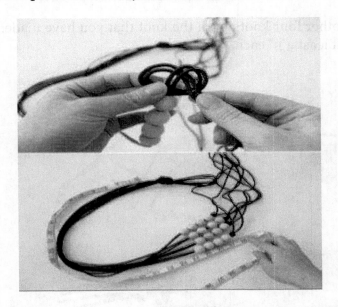

Look at the left set of the cord and tie it to the right string. Repeat on the four sets so that you could make at least 3" from the knot you have made.

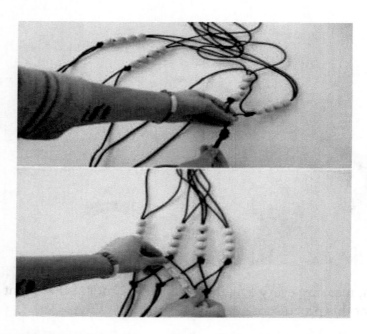

Tie another four knots from the knot that you have made. Make them at least 4.5" each.

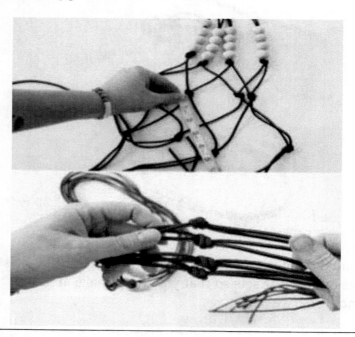

Group all of the cords together and tie a knot to finish the planter. You'll get something like the one shown below—and you could just add your very own planter to it!

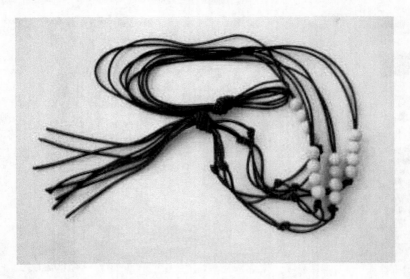

Amazing Macramé Curtain

Macramé Curtains give your house the feel of that beach house look. You don't even have to add any trinkets or shells—but you can, if you want to. Anyway, here's a great macramé Curtain that you can make!

What you need:

- Laundry rope (or any kind of rope/cord you want)

- Curtain rod

- Scissors
- Pins
- Lighter
- tape

Instructions:

Tie four strands together and secure the top knots with pins so they could hold the structure down.

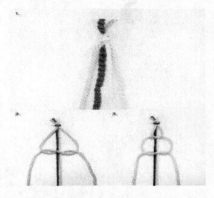

Take the strand on the outer right part and let it cross over to the left side by means of passing it through the middle. Tightly pull the strings together and reverse what you have done earlier.

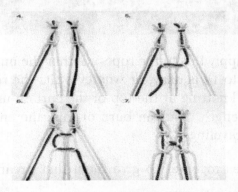

Repeat crossing the thread over four more times for the thread you now have in front of you. Take the strand on the outer left and let it pass through the middle, and then take the right and let it cross over the left side. Repeat as needed, then divide the group of strands to the left, and also to the right. Repeat until you reach the number of rows you want.

You can now apply this to the ropes. Gather the number of ropes you want—10 to 14 is okay, or whatever fits the rod, with good spacing. Start knotting at the top of the curtain until you reach your desired length. You can burn or tape the ends to prevent them from unraveling.

Braid the ropes together to give them that dreamy, beachside effect, just like what you see below.

That's it, you can now use your new curtain!

Macramé Charm and Feather Décor

Charms and feathers always look cool. They just add a lot of that enchanting feeling to your house and knowing that you could make macramé décor with charms and feathers really take your crafting game to new heights! Check out the instructions below and try it out for yourself!

What you need:

- Stick/dowel

- feathers and charms with holes (for you to insert the thread in)

- Embroidery/laundry rope (or any other rope or thread that you want)

Instructions:

Cut as many pieces of rope as you want. Around 10 to 12 pieces are good, and then fold each in half. Make sure to create a loop at each end, like the ones you see below:

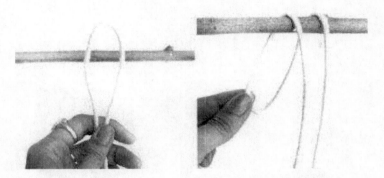

Then, go and loop each piece of thread on the stick.

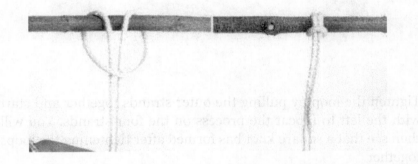

Make use of the square knot and make sure you have four strands for each knot. Let the leftmost strand cross the two strands and then put it over the strands that you have in the middle. Tuck it under the middle two, as well.

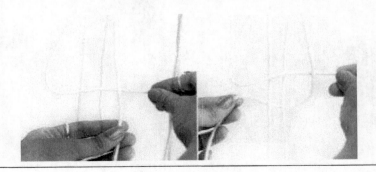

Check under the strands and let the rightmost strand be tucked under the loop to the left-hand strand.

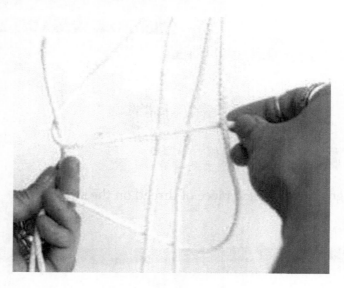

Tighten the loop by pulling the outer strands together and start with the left to repeat the process on the four strands. You will then see that a square knot has formed after tightening the loops together.

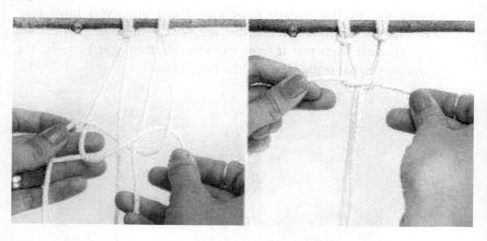

Connect the strands by doing square knots with the remaining four pieces of rope and then repeat the process again from the left side. Tighten the loop by pulling the outer strands together and start with the left to repeat the process on the four strands. You will then see that a square knot has formed after loops have been tightened together.

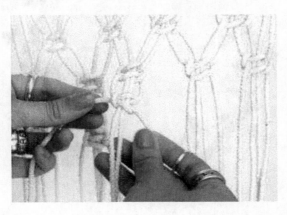

You can then do a figure-eight knot and then just attach charms and feathers to the end. Glue them in and burn the ends for better effect!

Wreath of Nature

Just imagine having a macramé wreath in your home! This one is inspired by nature and is one of the most creative things you could do with your time!

What you need:

- Clips or tape

- Fabric glue

- Wreath or ring frame

- 80 yards 12" cords

- 160 yards 17-18" cords

- 140 yards 14-16" cords

- 120 yards 12-13" cords

Instructions:

Mount the cords on top of the wreath and make the crown knot by folding one of the cords in half. Let the cords pass through the ring and then fold a knot and make sure to place it in front of the ring. Let the loops go over the ring and pull them your way so they could pass the area that has been folded.

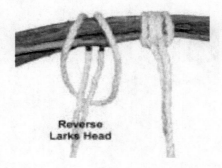

Reverse
Larks Head

Let the ends pass over the first loop so you could make way for some half-hitches. Let them go over and under the ring, and then tightly pull it over the cord. This way, you'd get something like the one below. Repeat these first few steps until you have mounted all the cords on top of the ring. Organize them in groups of ten.

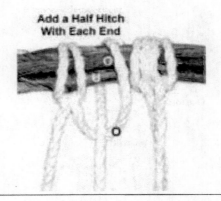

Add a Half Hitch
With Each End

Now, you can make leaf-like patterns. To do this, make sure to number the first group of cords on the right side and make half-hitches in a counterclockwise direction. Take note that you have to horizontally place the holding plate. If you see that it has curved slightly, make sure to reposition it and then attach cords labeled 5 to 7. Move it to resemble a diagonal position and then attach cords 8 to 10.

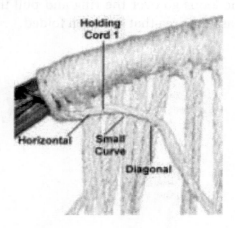

Make sure knots have been pushed close together and then use the cord on the leftmost corner to lower the leaf-like portion. The first four cords should be together on the handle and then go and attach cords labeled 3 to 6 to the holding cord. Move the cords so they'd be in a horizontal position.

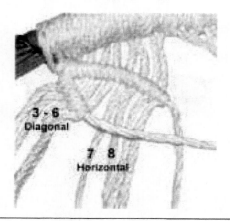

Now, move the cord upwards so that the center would not curve unnecessarily. Repeat the process for the cords on the bottom part of the frame and then start making the branches by selecting 2 to 4 cords from each of the leaves. Don't select the first and second row's first and last leaves.

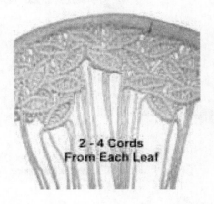

2 - 4 Cords
From Each Leaf

Hold the cords with tape or clips as you move them towards the back of the design and decide how you want to separate—or keep the branches together. Secure the cords with glue after moving them to the back.

Wrap the right cords around the ones on the left so that branches could be joined together. Make sure to use half-hitches to wrap this portion and then use a set of two cords to create a branch.

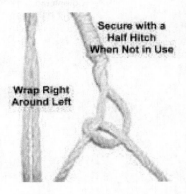

Secure with a
Half Hitch
When Not in Use

Wrap Right
Around Left

Let the branches intertwine by checking the plan you have written earlier and then use half-hitches again to connect the branches together. Together with your wrap, make use of another wrap and make sure they all come together as one.

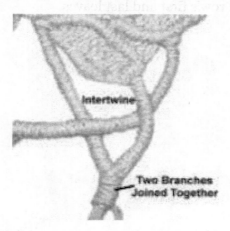

Secure the bundle by wrapping a 3-inch wrap cord around it and then let it go over the completed knot.

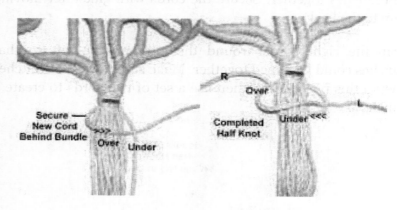

As for the fringe, you have to divide the knots into groups of two and make sure to tie a half-hitch on the rightmost cord on the leftover, and then let them alternate back and forth continuously until you have managed to cover the whole wreath. Let each sennit slide under the whole wreath and then attach each cord to the ring itself.

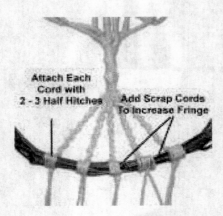

Make sure to divide the cords into small groups and then use the cords so you could tie the overhand knots. Unravel the fibers so you could form a wavy fringe.

That's it! You now have your own macramé Wreath of Nature!

Macramé Skirt Hanger

Well, it's not really a skirt hanger. But it's something that could spruce up your closet or your walls. It gives the room that dainty, airy feeling. You could also use it for plant pots that are at least 8 inches in size.

What you need:

- 12 mm size beads

- One 8-inch ring

- One 2-inch ring

- 4mm cord

Instructions:

First, cut 8 cords that are at least 8.5 yards long then cut a cord that is 36 inches long before cutting 4 more yards of cord.

Then, fold the 8.5 yards in half to start the top of the thread. Let it pass through the ring and let some parts drape down before choosing two cords from outside the bundle. Make sure to match the ends and then try the square knot.

To bundle the locks, you should find the center and move 8 inches down from it and then stop when you reach 12 inches.

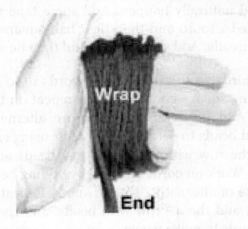

Wrap the center a couple of times and then pull the ends tightly until you build a sturdy bundle, and then tug on the ends so that the roll could get smaller.

Make a total of four spirals that could at least be 20 inches and then manage the filler cords by adding a bead to them.

To make the basket, attach the cords to the 8-inch ring by using double half-hitch stitches and then arrange the cords so they could be in four groups. Pull the stitches tightly so there's enough space and then mount all of the cords to the ring in a counterclockwise motion. To cover the ring, make sure to tie a half-hitch at each end.

Then, make alternating square knots just below the ring and divide into two groups of 40 strings each—it sounds like a lot but it's what would naturally happen. Add some tape to the cords you have labeled 1 to 40 and then tie a half-square knot to the four injected threads. Add some beads, and then tie a knot again.

Add beads to cords 20 to 21 after using cords 19 to 22 and then make alternating square knots and then repeat on the cords on the backside. Add beads and make more alternating square knots, then add beads to cords 16 to 17 after using cords labeled 15 to 18. Tie the row without adding any beads and then use cords 11 to 30. Work on cords 12 to 29 by adding beads to them and making use of alternating square knots. Repeat the 3rd row with no beads, and the 4th row with beads, and choose four of your favorite cords to make fringes.

Speaking of fringes, number the remaining cords mentally and then add a succession of 2 to 3 beads for each layer (i.e., 2/4/6 or 3/6/9) and then trim all the cords evenly.

Enjoy your new Skirt Hanger!

Going Beyond the Projects

Easy DIY Macramé Plant Holder

This is not the macramé of your grandma. All right, maybe it is, but at some point, something makes a comeback or another right? I love this macramé plant holder's smooth and textured feel. And the best part, the best part? It can be done in a few minutes! I'm all about basic projects that can be completed in a couple of minutes.

Macramé Plant Holder

This is a perfect project to make extra yarn scraps for friends and family. You can use live plants in its bowl, or you can use a fake one if you're a plant killer like me. Any watering? No watering? That's up my alley — let's start now!

Macramé Plant Holder Materials

- Metal or wooden ring

- Yarn

- Scissors

- Potted plant

Methods

1. Cut four different yarn lengths. Mine were about 2 feet long–you want to make sure that your plant holder is enough to finish! You may need to make the yarn strands even longer, depending on how big your plant is.

2. Fold half the strands of your yarn, then loop the folded end of your chain. Take the loose ends and pull them through the yarn loop you made.

3. Split the yarn into four yarn groups of two yarn strands each.

4. Measure several centimeters (I just looked at it) and tie each of the groups together. Ensure that the knots are about the same length.

5. Take the left path of each group and add it to the right path of the grouping. Keep the knots a little deeper, from the first set of knots only an inch or two. I know it sounds complicated, but it's not, I swear! Take the two external threads and bind them together to create a circular network.

6. Tie one additional round of knots, repeating the

process of knotting each group's left strand to the right strand. Bring the ties pretty close to the last round you made—just half or two inches away this time.

7. Tie all the threads of yarn a little under the last round of knots you made around one inch. Cut off the extra yarn to create a beautiful tassel!

Easy DIY Macramé Wall Hanging

A macramé wall suspended in a house

A macramé wall hanging is an easy DIY project which adds a handmade touch to every room in your house. Don't be afraid of turning it into your own.

Given its size, this is a simple project that takes you an hour or two to finish it. It gets together quickly, and you will find many ways of adding your style.

This is only one of many free macramé patterns including plant hangers, curtains, and much more.

The knots you use to mount this macramé wall include the head knot, the spiral knot, and the square knot.

What you will need to finish this macramé DIY hanging wall:

Cotton macramé cord (200 feet) and 61 meters (3/4-inch circumference, 24) "wooden dowel" (3/4, 24-inch) scissors I've been using cotton clothesline on my macramé string. It looks entirely natural and it is quite cheap.

The wooden dowel must not be such exact measurements and use whatever scale you like in place of the wooden dowel as long as all ropes are placed over it. If you want to give it an outdoor experience, you can use a branch of a tree about the same height.

Make a Hanger for Your Wooden Dowel

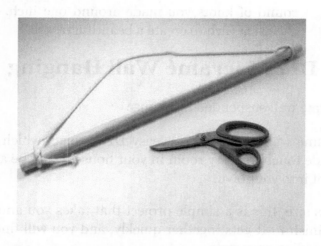

Cut a piece of macramé cord that is three feet (1 meter) and tie it to the wooden dowel. Connect the two sides of the wooden dowel to each end of the thread. You are going to use this to mount your macramé project when it is over. In the beginning, I like to attach it, so I can hang up the macramé project when I tie knots. It is much easier to work this way than to determine it.

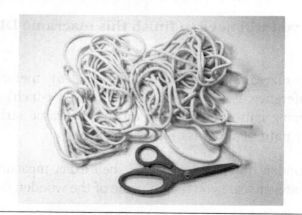

Cut your macramé rope into 12 string lengths 15 feet (4.5 meters) long with a pair of scissors. It might sound like a lot of rope, but knots take up more cord than you expect. If you need it, there's no way to make the rope thicker, so you better cut it than you will.

Fold one of the macramé cores in half on the wooden dowel and use a ladle's head knot to tie it to a wooden dowel.

Join the other cords in the same way

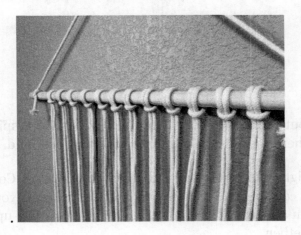

Take the first four strings and make left facing spiral stitch (also referred to as a half-knot Lynton) by tying 13 half knots.

Using four rope to make a further spiral stitch of 13 half knots using the same pair of four ropes. Continue to work in four-chord. You should have a minimum of six spiral stitches before you finish.

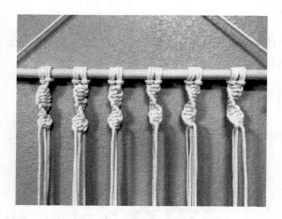

Scale about two inches down from the last knot in a spiral point. This is where your knot, the square knot, will be found.

Make a right knot profile with the first four strings. Continue to make the correct knots face throughout this row. Do your best to keep them all even horizontally. You're going to end up with six knots together.

The second row of square knots, now it is the time to start the square knots so we can have the knots "V" shape

Set open the first two strings and the last two strings. Consider each group of four right-facing square knots. You now have a second line with the first two and last two unknotted cords and six square knots. It doesn't matter how you space them; just keep them for each row together.

Keep Decreasing the Square knots. A "V" formed from the square knots in the third row, the first four strings, and the last four strings will be left out. You're going to have four knots together. For the fourth row at the top, leave six cords and at the end six cords. You're going to have 3 square ties. In the fifth row, in the beginning, you'll have eight cords and at the end eight cords. Now you're going to have two square ties. For the sixth and final row, ten cords at the beginning and ten cords at the end are to be released. It lets you make a last square knot with four strings.

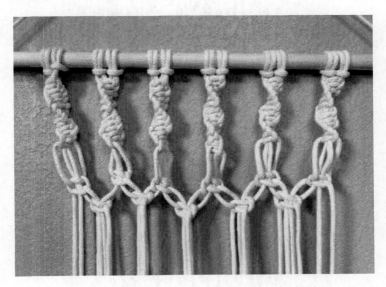

Square Knots Square Making a second "V" in square knots time we'll increase them into a triangle or an upside-down" V "For this first segment, bring out the first eight and last eight cords. That will make two square knots.

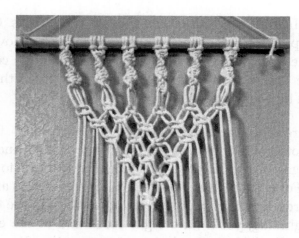

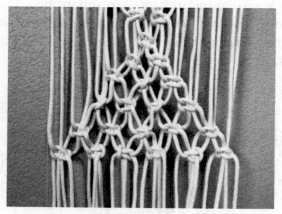

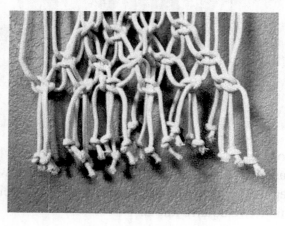

You already know the term macramé whether you grew up in the 1970s or have been on Pinterest for several years. Macramé models have elaborated designs with a variety of knots that come in different shapes and sizes.

The most common examples on the internet are wall hangings, but with this technique and material, you can do much more. And while we're still looking forward to one of these exciting projects, we have decided to move the focus away from the wall and to more practical concepts.

These macramé tutorials are great for beginners and some of them can be completed with a single node. The demo lacks nodes but uses a macramé cord to twist. Would you like to learn more? See the favorite examples below.

Nonetheless, first, learn how to make a few simple macramé knots before you launch any of the following projects. Practice these knots until you are confident in the result as much as possible.

A Macramé Table Runner

A Beautiful Mess Most macramé table runners are out there, but we love that by A Beautiful Mess. The photos break the pattern into simple steps, and the instructions are straightforward. It can be challenging to figure out how to make a knot without a recording, but these pictures give you a good idea of what every knot will look like.

I talk in layers of co-ordination and contrasts when decorating every room. Such three elements that make a room less simple, regardless of whether it is color, texture, or scale. My fourth guideline is polyvalence! This macramé table runner checked all boxes and made this compact nook with its basic and intriguing style even more unique.

All you need to know is three essential nodes, and you have a charming layer that works every season. If you know the knots learned here, you can tailor your table runner to the length of your table or change it totally and create a hanging macramé wall.

Supply: -12″ wooden dowel −22 lengths of cotton rope measuring 3 mm −with cotton twine over the door−2″ with dowel hanger scissors

- **Step One:** Apply cotton twine to each end of the dowel and hang it on the door hanger. Fold your first 16″ rope strand in half and create a knot on your dowel.

- **Step Two:** Keep each 16′ rope strand with a lark's head knot until you have a total of 22. This will allow you to work with 44 strands.

- **Step 3:** Cast the outside right strands across all the other strands (left) and drop the end of your door handle. This will form the basis of the series of knots known as a half-hitch to create a horizontal row. Use the second rope from the right side to tie a knot around the rope you have just draped so that it's 6″ below the dowel.

- **Step Four:** Use the same beach to tie a second knot to the foundation line. This is regarded as a halving knot.

- **Step Five:** Make sure they are clear and even.

- **Step Six:** Repeat from the outside with the second, third, and fourth ropes and tie another hitch-knot, so it is snug, etc. You're going to begin to see the trend. It's a half-hitch horizontal.

- **Step 7:** Continue to tie successive cords throughout a single knot. You don't want to be so close that it's at the edges in the distance.

- **Step 8:** From the right again, use the four outer strands to build a knot about 1.5″ below the horizontal knots. See this macramé storage article for more information on a square knot.

Out the four (five to eight) strands then tie another knot of nine to twelve strands. Keep skipping four before you cross the line.

- **Step Nine:** Begin again on the right, use the four strands that you skipped (five to eight) and tie a square knot about 3″ below the dowel.

- **Step Ten:** Continue tying four-strand sets in square knots until the row is ended.

Materials Source List

Natural Materials

Natural materials for macramé are still very common choices. They have properties that are very different from conventional materials that you need to know if you want to use them. This contains a description of today's most common natural cord materials. And yarns made from natural fibers, too.

Hemp Material

Hemp twine is the most common of all the natural products used for macramé. The natural color here in the back is light brown. Dyed hemp comes in colors that are single or mixed. Hemp products are produced from the outer bark of the plant genus Cannabis Sativa, one of the fastest-growing plants. This crop was first woven into fiber 10,000 years ago, sometimes called "Industrial Hemp." Generally, plants do not require chemicals or pesticides, making it one of today's cleanest natural materials. Fiber materials include paper, clothes, biodegradable plastics, food, paint, and biofuel.

- **There are three types of hemp:** Twine, rope, and yarn. They each have different properties, so I'll separately explain them.

  Hemp Rope usually has a diameter of 1 mm to 3 mm and is determined by size instead of weight. Size 3mm is sometimes referred to as "Spring Cord" because it is often used in spring mattress construction.

- **Properties:**

  Hemp fibers are mold and mildew resistant, which

makes them distinct from other natural materials.

Hemp "yarn" is solid and so flexible, but not like knitting yarn. In the way this bends, it is similar to cotton. This creates perfect solid knots keeping their form.

For strong knot designs, Hemp "twine" is just as flexible and it is a good choice.

Hemp "cord" is less flexible, and when you use it you can find it difficult to tie some knots.

Hemp "twine" is made of many fibers as well, but usually, it has more than the thread. It can be found in different colors and patterns.

Hemp "cord" begins as a yarn, made of several twisted fibers. The yarns are then twisted to form the cord together. So, it is double twisted, which makes it much more effective. It is not easy to find and is usually a natural brown color.

Cotton Materials

Cotton cord remains one of the most common natural materials for macramé and related crafts. It's a very clean fiber, and hypoallergenic. Cotton fibers are easy to dye, so the materials come in many colors. The natural color is creamy white. Cotton is currently the world's most used natural fiber. Every part of the plant can be used in some manner. The short fibers (lint) are used to make paper and medical supplies. Seeds are used for the production of food (cotton oil), cosmetics, color, candle, soap, etc.

- **Properties:**

Cotton is the most versatile of all the natural materials

used in macramé. You can use it for big items like hammocks and fine jewelry suspensions. Cotton is the softest of all-natural fabrics. But, one thing people don't like is that it can be a bit fluffy, depending on your style. It's a very strong and flexible cotton cord. It may be washed and dried, but it may be diminishing. Handbags and clothes from macramé should be hand washed and air-dried. This material creates strong ties that are uniform. There is very little stretching, which is important to hold weight when making items. Cotton intensity improves when it is wet. Yet that's not how it should stay, because it's going to get rotten. Sunlight affects cotton, which can make the color yellow and cause it to degrade. Hold the material protected and check the material periodically for signs of rot or cracking when using the material for outdoor products.

Jute Twine

Jute twine is the least common of all the natural materials available for macramé. Finding a good quality Jute material is very hard, it is going to be the same width in the roll. It'll be cool, too, with a little shine. Jute is a plant with a high content of cellulose and wood fiber. It is woven into compressed and twisted coarse threads to form cords. Many Jute fiber fabrics are used to make inexpensive burlap bags, carpets, chairs, canvas, etc. Often jute fibers are mixed with other materials for making clothes and household furniture. One thing people like is the blurred quality of it. Jute's going to have SMALL tendrils in good quality. Colored Jute is difficult to find, but online shops carrying packaging can have it.

- **Size:**

The natural materials are also sold by the number of fibers that make up the PLY cord. With Jute, ply and weight define the sizes, making it very confusing. The scale of the producer also varies.

- **Properties:**

This course content, even in the heavyweight format, is strong and surprisingly flexible. The weights of the medium make strong knots. The heavyweight will take more effort, but the knots will still be fairly tight. Jute's strength will decrease if it's muddy. This is also quickly biodegrading. That's why this isn't the perfect choice for outdoor projects. Finding good quality content is the most difficult thing with the Jute cord.

Linen Cord

Linen cord is a special Flax plant fiber. It's not as common as other natural materials. Because it is mainly used for jewelry, it is often carried by online stores. The cellulose fibers just below the bark of the flax (stem) plant are collected first, then spun into threads and yarns. We then make clothes, bedding, and household things.

This ancient fiber has been used for producing silk since 3,000 BC. It was finer and more luxurious than anything in current use back then. Until burial, Egyptian Kings were covered with Flax fabric strips. It was highly appreciated by Greeks and Romans, and it was considered sacred. It takes time and effort to harvest and process the fiber so that only a few countries produce it for commercial purposes.

- **Size:**

Sadly, it is difficult to find linen in the form of cord or yarn without living in the producer countries. It is provided by Ireland, Belgium, and Scotland, along with several other countries in the vicinity. It is often called

"Irish Linen" when you find this material it is usually between 0.6 mm and 2 mm in diameter. The PLY markets it, varying from 2-ply to 8-ply.

- **Properties:**

Flax Linen is the most powerful of all-natural plant materials. This is unique because when wet, it is stronger. It can last without deterioration for hundreds of years. Its anti-static properties help to withstand stain and dust.

- **Style:**

Flax linen cord is normally a material of twist style. These are highly flexible, producing tight knots. Usually, the natural colors are gray, yellow-gold, or brown. It can also be used in several colors. A waxed cord of linen is a great beading and micro-macramé option. Flax cord material, similar to lacing, may often have a flat profile. For this style, you can still tie knots, but you have to work a bit more for the cord so these folds and bends easily.

Silk Cord

It is possible to produce natural products from animals. Moth larvae originating in northern China are produced from soil called Silkworm. Every cocoon is made of 1,000 – 2,000 feet long, continuous thread of raw silk filament. Silk has been used in clothing, art, and decorations in ancient China. Back then, as it is now, it was a luxury material. Creating 1 yard/meter of fabric requires around 3,000 coconuts. Instead of their increased cost after World War 2, synthetic materials were created to replace silk. Several countries still produce genuine silk, but it is still expensive.

- **Properties:**

Silk is the most powerful of all-natural materials. It has a shiny, but not slippery, soft texture. Typically, it stays that way if the cord/thread is extended. When wet, or exposed to sunlight for long periods, it is weakened. Silk is delicate, given its strength. So, when dealing with it, using the cross-pin method (or no pins at all). You may also roll and stitch the seed to form the cord.

Leather Cord

Leather is made of animals as well. This has somewhat different characteristics than other natural materials. Cattle are primarily raised for food, but all parts, including the hide, are used. Leather is made of hides and skins in different shapes. To avoid decomposition, leather is tanned. This is done using some ingredients, many of which are natural products such as tree bark and leaves. With brains or other fatty substances, buckskin is tanned. Chromium is the most common chemicals used for tanning. Leather is stabilized, thin, lubricated after tanning. This is known as crusting. It may be done in various ways, gently painted.

Not all leather is made of cattle: Fish Leather is made of fish species ' skin and scales. Deerskin Leather is made of skins of deer. Pig, Elephant, Alligator, Lizard, Squirrel, Ostrich, Kangaroo, Leather from other species.

- **Size**

   Leather cord comes in so many sizes, but if it's longer than 2 mm, it's really hard to make knots. The best jewelry size is between 1 mm and 1.5 mm.

- **Properties:**

   Leather is incredibly strong, but very fragile as well. It is important, because the holes are permanent, that you do not pass pins through the material. To secure the cords to a project board, use the cross-pin technique or tape. The cord of leather on the skin is very smooth and comfortable. It's not very good at breathing so you should use your designs as little as you can. The natural color of bovine leather is brown, but in many colors, you can also get it. The shape of the knots is better in leather than any other cord material. Also, loosely bound knots will maintain their form, like those that produce up this Leather Bracelet. Similar to other natural materials, leather is not versatile. Tightening knots with material over 2 mm long is very difficult. That's the biggest reason why it doesn't make big macramé items.

Natural Yarns

Natural materials include different types of yarn that can be used for projects in macramé.

- **Size:**

    Most yarns are priced by weight, so it's difficult to assess the material's actual width before you get it and measure it. Just a few brands will show the actual width so quantity in the roll on the label. Keep in mind that the yarn is so compact that the knots are smaller than expected.

Normally wool yarn can be stretched, and when released, this will spring back. The material repels moisture and is therefore flammable. Merino Wool is extra soft, not as scratchy as other wool yarn types.

Alpaca yarn is cool and finer than wool. It's not prickly either, or it doesn't have lanolin. It is also considered to be hypoallergenic. Some brands are brilliant.

It is not necessary to make natural materials from animals. Paper yarn is made of a wide variety of paper products, including rice paper, washi, and raffia. These are fuzz-free fabrics that are easy to dye.

Bamboo yarn is another special kind of natural fiber made from the bamboo plant's pulp. It's strong, very flexible, and it can be as soft as silk. It's got a perfect natural shine. It makes very tight, tiny knots. Pins will damage bamboo yarn, so treat it as if you were going to use some fragile material and use the cross-Pin Technique or no pins at all.

For any kind of yarn, tape is not recommended.

Synthetic Materials

For macramé projects, synthetic materials are commonly used. Olefin, parachute cord, nylon beading cord, and satin cord are the common synthetic materials. Different sizes, general and specific properties, available styles, and price range are included.

"Synthetic" means that the fibers are made by a chemical process.

"Natural" means that the fibers are made of animals or plants. Such materials are explained in the context of "natural materials."

The Basic Crochet Stitches

Slip Stitch

The starting stitch to practice on is the slip stitch which is a look-alike of the single crochet stitch. It is necessary to connect the rounds, join squares, and edging to finish items off neatly. Get ready to try your first slip stitch.

Place a loop on your crochet hook, follow by slowly sticking in the hook into the place where you want the slip stitch to be. Then simply hook the yarn around your needle.

Now you can pull the yarn through and you can pull the new loop through after the active loop which you already have on your hook.

Try this a few times and before you know it, you'll be doing it in your sleep. You have finished your first slip stitch. The slip stitch is useful for the following:

Forming a Crochet Ring

Some patterns start by creating a ring in the center. Common examples are granny squares and hexagons. Patterns such as these often begin with a few chain stitches that you'll need to join to create a ring. The slip stitch is what joins the two ends.

It is simple to make a ring shape in crocheting. Stick in the crochet hook to the end of the chain and crochet a slip stitch.

Join Round with a Slip Stitch

Once you have completed around, there is likely to be a gap between the beginning and the end. The slip stitch is used to close the gap and join the rounds. It is commonly used when working granny squares.

If you are using a pattern, it will indicate whether or not you should do this. You may not need to work a slip stitch at all, particularly if your rounds are worked in a spiral.

It is possible to work a slip stitch on the surface of any crocheted fabric. Slip stitches are great for embellishing your crochet items. You can also use them to outline shapes and designs to give them a pop of color.

An easy way of doing this is to cut out a design, pin it on the surface and then work your slip stitch around it. You can mark the design effectively using this method. If you prefer, you can also use a fabric marker to draw the outline.

Joining Crocheted Elements Using a Slip Stitch

Slip stitches are suitable for joining crochet elements. For example, you can use this stitch to join your crocheted squares or even stitch up the seams on a pattern you are using. A slip stitch is usually suitable for joining any crocheted pieces. When joining two pieces together, along the edges as you work each slip stitch.

Chain Stitch

Following the slip stitch, this is usually the first stitch you'll create as part of a long chain. Chain stitches are an important foundation from which beautiful creations can be made. Crochet patterns often include chain stitches amongst the other stitches as part of the design. While you are practicing your chain stitch, focus on keeping your tension as consistent as you can and holding your crochet hook correctly.

Take your hook with your right hand and hold in the same manner that you would a pencil or a knife, as long as you feel confident. As you begin, the hook should be facing upwards and as you crochet each chain stitch, you'll need to your hook slightly in a counterclockwise direction.

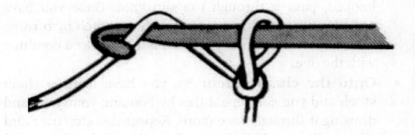

- **Crocheting of the first stitch:** At this point, you place the hook inside of the slip knot you just made. You should loop the yarn steadily over your hook. This should be done from the back through to the front. To makes this slightly easier you can try holding your slip knot using the tip of your index finger.

As the crochet hook remains in the slip knot, all you have to do is loop over the yarn from the back to the front. It may help by holding on to the slip knot on the hook with your index finger. Turn the crochet hook as you loop over the yarn to the hook.

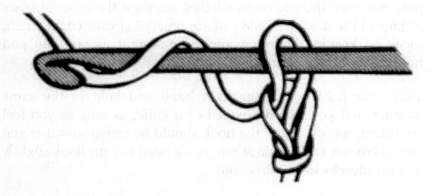

- **Forming the First Chain Stitch:** Once the yarn is hooked, pass it through the slip knot. Once you have pulled your yarn out, you can finish the stitch by turning the hook to its original position so that you can continue with the one.
- **Onto the chain stitch:** So, you have made a chain stitch and you can repeat this by hooking your yarn and drawing it through once more. Repeat this step over and over until your chain is complete. Your index finger and thumb can be used to hold your chain stitches as you lengthen the chain.

In time, you'll be able to work rhythmically as you rotate the crochet hook so that you can hook the yarn and then draw it out once again.

- **Some useful tips:** Tips for Making a Foundation Chain

- **Counting stitches:** As you count your chain, exclude the slip knot and start at the first chain stitch.

- **Do what works for you:** There are many positions in which you can hold your hook and yarn as you work. Try these according to the instructions and feel free to change your position slightly if it makes it easier for you.

- **An even tension:** Keep practicing until you get your tension right and your stitches are not too loose or too tight.

Single

This stitch is vital as it is used in so many crochet patterns and is so easy to do. You can do so much with it. Whether you are working in rows, spirals, or rounds. It is also perfect for edging and combining other stitches. So, let's get to it, shall we?

- **Inserting the crochet hook:** Once your chain is done, stick your hook in through your first Ch stitch. For the following row, you should put your hook into the single crochet stitch which lies beneath it in the row, and so on.

Slide your hook under both loops which lie at the top of the chain. (Some patterns work through one loop at a time)

- **The soon step is to yarn over and grip the yarn:** Draw a loop through and circle your yarn over your hook, and then pass it through with the hook.

You'll see 2 stitches that appear as loops.

- **Repeat yarn over:** Circle the yarn around the hook as before, and then hook it.

Pass the yarn through the two of the loops in one step.

Your single crochet stitch is done. As you finish, you'll have only one loop remaining which serves as the insert for your stitch.

To finish a row of single crochet stitches then all you have to do is simply repeat the steps as needed.

- **Just a hint:** It can be difficult holding your work while stitching rows, the first row in particular. So, if it seems as if you are struggling, don't be discouraged, you'll get the hang of it. If you have someone who can do the first few rows for you, it will be easier for you to continue from there because it will be easier to hold it than a row which is still to be worked.

Once you are comfortable with the single crochet stitch,

you can try doing the first few rows on your own. It will get easier, and you need to master this as you will need it in the future.

Variations of Single Crochet

You can change the look of a pattern by making simple variations of a single crochet stitch. Here are a few ideas.

Insert your hook so that it enters the front loop only (FLO) of the stitch on the top right-hand side. This is an open style of this stitch.

Insert your hook so that it enters the back loop only (BLO) of the stitch on the bottom left-hand side. This results in a stretchy ribbed look which is a rather popular variation.

You may insert your hook in different positions, but your technique remains the same so that you can create simple variations of the single crochet. Using these will enable you to make beautiful, dense fabrics with which to create scarves and blankets if you so wish. These are useful items and canal be made using a single crochet stitch.

The Double Crochet

The double crochet is another important basic stitch and is one of the foundational stitches, although it can easily be excluded from many simple patterns. You can use this stitch on its own by working rows or rounds and it is popular in many common stitch patterns such as the granny square, which is a classic, as well as the v-stitch.

These instructions enable you to practice on your own until you are confident with using this stitch.

- One has to begin with one stitch on their hook and then

they should wrap the yarn over the hook of their needle.

- Insert your hook into the stitch. If you start with a foundation chain, stick your hook into your fourth stitch.

- Then circle the yarn over the hook again so that your hook passes through the yarn.

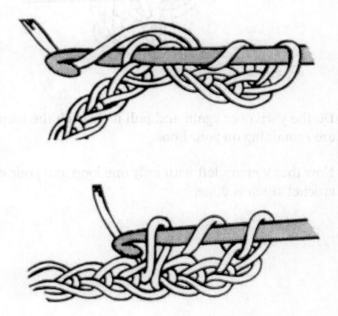

You should circle your yarn over the same way that you

did it when you inserted your hook the first time. However, now you'll have more yarn on the crochet hook and it might seem slightly more difficult than it did earlier. It takes time to get it right.

- There should be three loops left.

- Repeat yarn over and draw it through.

- Encircle the yarn over the hook once more and then pass it through the two loops nearest to the end of the hook.

- Now there are some 2 loops on the hook.

- Do the yarn over again and pull it through the loops that are remaining on your hook.

- Now that you are left with only one loop and your double crochet stitch is done.

You can build a rhythm as you practice this stitch so that you can yarn over and pass it through your loops, it will seem like one step.

Double crochet hint:

- The easiest way to practice this stitch is by working it in a straight row. You can stick in the hook to the bottom of these two loops under your stitch.

- For patterns that include spaces, like the granny square, you can do the following: Insert your hook into space beneath the stitch you are working rather than into the loops. It is best to practice using regular rows and then go on learning how to work a double crochet into spaces.

- You may have to work your double crochet into a different stitch. There are several variations of double crochet. However, the basics of working double crochet stitches into rows will enable you to use any patterns.

Crochet Tips and Tricks

1. To avoid balls of yarn from falling and rolling, place them in a reused hand wipe jar of cylindrical shape. Just like wipes, the yarn will also come out through the same hole.

2. Mark your rows by using a stitch marker, bobby pin, safety pin.

3. Store your crochet hooks in the jewelry box, pencil box, or traveling toothpaste holder. You can also hang your hooks on a small piece of wool. A multipurpose storage box is also a good option.

4. Highlight your pattern with different colors so that you can understand it easily. Underline different stitches. If your patterns demand rows of a different color, highlight the rows with the same color or with the colors that you have decided to use.

5. Always keep abbreviations, measurements, hook, and yarn weights table in printable forms so that you can easily use them whenever you want.

6. Use rapped or leftover yarns to make pom poms, Afghan squares, bracelets, and many more articles like these.

7. If you use the homespun yarn for your pattern, then metal hooks are a better option than plastic ones.

8. If you love to do crochet during traveling, prepare a separate crochet box. Always have travel-friendly crochet tools, for example, foldable scissors that are easy to carry and also will not snug the things in the bag.

9. Many crochet patterns do not go well with ironing. So instead of it, take an equal quantity of water and starch

and spray the pattern with it and let it dry on a flat surface.

10. Store the crochet patterns in your notebook by using sheet protectors.

11. Make sure you sit in a proper position to provide enough support to your elbows, and hands during crocheting.

12. Take breaks after regular intervals to refresh yourself.

13. There is a variety of hand massage and stretching techniques. So, do any of them that you find it easy to relax your hand muscles.

14. Using ergonomic crochet tools such as circular needles is also useful to avoid hand fatigue.

15. Use stress relief gloves.

16. Pick up your hook every day. The hardest part about learning how to crochet is training your hand to hold your hook (and the yarn) with the correct tension. At first, it feels a little awkward and unnatural but if you make it a habit of picking up your hook every day when you are first learning the craft; it will become easy in no time. Do not give up and keep in mind that practice makes perfect!

17. Begin with small projects. Learning how to crochet takes time and most of the time, beginners feel discouraged when they are not able to complete a project – I mean, who wouldn't? The best thing to do is to start with small attainable projects. There is no better feeling than completing your very own first project. Start with small items such as squares, mandalas, and coasters before moving onto larger projects such as blankets and

cushions

18. Chain, chain, chain. When learning to crochet, making several chains is the best way to improve your tension since they are the foundation of all stitches. You will be ready for stitches that are more complicated once all your chains look nice and even

Mistakes Crochets Make and Solution

As a beginner, you must come across your fair share of frustrations as you get stuck into your crocheting. Mistakes could happen by not following instructions accurately, or simply as a result of lack of practice. Remember, there are certain methods you can adjust slightly to suit you, as long as they don't affect the appearance of your stitches and your pattern.

Learning to crochet can be a wonderful experience, so try not to get too despondent if you don't always manage to do everything properly at first. It is a very time-consuming craft and requires a lot of skill which you will develop over time. Don't be too hard on yourself and just have fun.

1. Inserting your hook into the wrong chain when you start

Don't count the first chain on the hook because it is just a loop, your first proper chain is the first chain from the hook which is the one to and the one after that is the second loop on the hook.

Check when you use US stitches and when your pattern contains UK pattern terms. This can sometimes be easy to miss and cause several complications. An easy way to check is to look out for single crochet instruction as this confirms that your pattern is a US pattern that uses US terminology.

2. Not considering blocking as an important step

First of all, blocking involves hand washing an item and then pinning it into place on a blocking mat. The reason for doing this is to straighten the item and flatten it if needed. It is possible to machine wash your item, just use the hand setting. There are times when blocking isn't completely necessary, whereas so for you. If you intend to wash it then be sure to use the blocked gauge measurements.

3. Making starting loops using linked chains and not a magic loop

You could use methods of starting your crocheting in the round. The first is to work four or five chain stitches and join them in a circle by using a slipstitch. This is the simplest method.

4. Not changing the size of your hook as needed

You may have done this and only realized it when your work didn't look quite right. This can happen when your starting chain is rather tight in comparison to the rest of your work. This is, however, a common mistake among beginners. You must have the right tension in your chain as it forms the foundation of your work.

One solution is to use a slightly larger hook than recommended in your pattern as this will help you to have a more even tension throughout. It is not necessary to change the size of your hook if your tension is correct. Always be aware of specific crochet hook sizes on your patterns.

5. Your work seems to be shrinking

If you find that your work is shrinking in places and the shape of your item doesn't look right, then you have probably made an error somewhere. The explanation for a mistake such as this is usually a result of making your first stitch in the incorrect position.

Remember these points:

- For single crochet, the first stitch is inserted into the first stitch of the row above.

- For your other basic stitches, it is the turning chain which is to be counted as the first stitch. Hence, this first stitch is inserted into what is the second one of the rows.

6. Not being able to identify your stitches

It is common for beginners to be so involved in trying to follow the instructions in their patterns that they seldom check to see whether their stitches look the way they should. Never fear, this is quite normal and a mistake made by so many of us. There are lots of different moving parts and it takes a while to catch your rhythm. When you first start crocheting, take a moment to count your stitches and learn what they look like.

7. Avoiding new techniques because they seem too difficult.

If something seems too difficult, look at it more carefully before avoiding it completely. If you can do the basic stitches, you'll be able to handle nearly all the crochet techniques without any problem. You may just need to practice a few times. The steps can sometimes seem a bit intimidating, but if you read through them, you'll see that they are made up of basic instructions. So, don't avoid trying something new, it may be easier than you think, and you'll be able to take your crochet to a new level before you know it!

8. Not learning enough about yarn

When you start buying yarns, learn as much as you can about them. You will, of course, have to use certain yarns depending on the patterns you are using. But also try and find out which ones are of good quality and don't always go for the cheapest.

You don't realize that your turning chain is the same height as the first stitch in the row.

You should be able to see that the starting chain of your row brings the height of your work up to that of the first stitch in that row. For example, single crochet is one chain and half double crochet is two chains. Have a look at this the time you are crocheting.

9. Not being able to read patterns

Nowadays, one can tend to be a little bit lazy when it is about reading patterns. This is because online videos are much quicker and easier to follow for some of us. However, this is not ideal, as one should be able to read patterns. By reading through the pattern steps, you'll be able to create a picture in your mind of what the pattern should look like and it will give you a better understanding of what you are doing.

10. Not learning corner-to-corner (C2C) crochet

The C2C method is an important and useful one to learn. You will most definitely use it many times and it is great for making blankets and other garments. Don't avoid this one, try it and practice, you won't be sorry for doing it.

11. Not learning how to crochet in the round

It is important to see how this works and then try it. This is vital to improving your crochet skills, so don't put off learning how to crochet in the round. It is a valuable technique to know how to use.

12. Not learning how to weave in ends properly

This is one of the most common mistakes made by beginners. It is so easy to just tie knots to the ends, but this is not the proper way of doing it and it is not neat either. Learn to weave the ends into the surface by using the tapestry needle to finish your work.

13. Worrying about your mistakes

Making mistakes is what helps you to learn and improve your work. Lots of practice and even more patience, as well as some creativity, is what makes a successful crochet. You will have to undo your stitches from time to time, or even start over again, but that is fine. You are not only learning how to follow instructions; you are also getting used to using your tools and materials so be patient.

14. Trying out complex patterns first

So often, ladies are in a hurry to create the most beautiful colorful garments without being able to master the stitches or change their yarn colors. This could result in a disaster which could also be incredibly discouraging. Just keep it simple until you are confident with basic crochet work.

15. Giving up too soon

It is too easy to just pick up your crochet hook, try out a few stitches, and then give up if they don't work. You might feel as though you are getting nowhere, but that is not true. Give yourself plenty of time to learn the basics because once you can do that, then you can move forward and make so many items. If you cannot get your basic stitches right, then you will have problems making your item. Take it easy and things will slowly start coming together.

Even the most skillful people struggled at first, so go for it and enjoy it!

Conclusion

Well done!

The beauty of macramé as a vintage art that has survived extinction for centuries and has continued to thrive as a technique of choice for making simple but sophisticated items is simply unrivaled. The simple fact that you have decided to read this manual means that you are well on your way to making something great. There is truly a certain, unequaled feeling of satisfaction that comes from crafting your own masterpiece.

The most important rule in macramé is the maxim: "Practice makes perfect." If you cease to practice constantly, your skills are likely to deteriorate over time. So, keep your skills sharp, exercise the creative parts of your brain, and keep creating mind-blowing handmade masterpieces.

Jewelry and fashion accessories made with even the most basic macramé knots are always a beauty to behold; hence they serve as perfect gifts for loved ones on special occasions. Presenting a macramé bracelet to someone, for instance, passes the message that you didn't just remember to get them a gift, you also treasure them so much that you chose to invest your time into crafting something unique especially for them too, and trust me, that is a very powerful message.

However, the most beautiful thing about macramé is perhaps the fact that it helps to create durable items. Hence you can keep a piece of decoration, or a fashion accessory you made for yourself for many years, enjoy the value, and still feel nostalgic anytime you remember when you made it. It even feels better when you made that item with someone. This feature of durability also makes macramé accessories incredibly perfect gifts.

Macramé can also serve as an avenue for you to begin your dream small business. After perfecting your macramé skills, you can conveniently sell your items and get paid well for your products, especially if you can perfectly make items like bracelets that people buy a lot. You could even train people and start your own small business that makes custom macramé fashion accessories. The opportunities macramé presents are truly endless.

So, stay sharp, keep practicing, and keep getting better. Welcome to a world of infinite possibilities!

Stop reading, start doing!

Printed by BoD™in Norderstedt, Germany